AUTISM QUICK GUIDE FOR TUTORS

NICHOLAS CRANK

Table of Contents

Introduction

I understand that diving into the complexities of the autism spectrum can be a challenging but deeply rewarding journey, especially when you're working with autistic learners. As someone who's dedicated to making a positive impact on their lives, it's essential to have a thorough grasp of the spectrum.

The autism spectrum isn't a monolithic entity; it's a beautifully diverse range of characteristics and experiences. It's like a mosaic, with each piece representing an individual's unique strengths and challenges.

In my experience, I've come to appreciate that the spectrum spans from individuals who may face severe challenges in communication and social interaction to those who possess incredible talents and abilities in specific areas. It's a broad spectrum that encompasses a multitude of colors, shades, and patterns.

We must remember that autism isn't just about challenges; it's also about celebrating the strengths and exceptional abilities that many autistic individuals possess. They might excel in mathematics, music, art, or have a remarkable eye for detail. It's our privilege to recognize and nurture these talents.

Autism is not a one-size-fits-all concept. It's about understanding, supporting, and embracing the uniqueness of each learner. This journey will be filled with moments of joy and accomplishment, but it may also come with its share of challenges. Together, we can navigate this path with empathy, patience, and the knowledge that we're making a profound difference in the lives of these remarkable individuals. Let's embark on this journey together, celebrating the beauty of neurodiversity and the potential that lies within each autistic learner.

Chapter 1: Understanding Autism

An In-Depth Look at the Spectrum

I understand that you're looking for a deep dive into the autism spectrum, and I'm here to provide you with a comprehensive understanding. The autism spectrum is a rich tapestry of experiences, characteristics, and challenges that span a wide range. It's important to approach this topic with empathy and an open heart because the spectrum isn't a single, uniform entity. It's a diverse and multifaceted landscape.

At its core, the autism spectrum is defined by certain key features. These include differences in communication, social interaction, and the presence of repetitive behaviors or intense interests. But it's the unique combination and intensity of these features that create the vast spectrum we see in the autism community.

Let's break down the spectrum into several important aspects:

1. Communication Differences: Autism often manifests as variations in communication. Some individuals may struggle with spoken language, relying on alternative methods such as non-verbal communication or augmentative and alternative communication (AAC). Others may have advanced language skills but face challenges in understanding and using language in a social context.

2. Social Interaction: Difficulty in social interactions is a common hallmark of autism. It can range from challenges in understanding social cues and norms to a profound struggle in forming and maintaining relationships. However, it's crucial to recognize that there's a wide spectrum within this domain.

3. Repetitive Behaviors: Repetitive behaviors and rituals can be a part of an autistic individual's life. These behaviors can range from simple hand-flapping to more complex rituals. Understanding the purpose and function of these behaviors is key to providing effective support.

4. Sensory Sensitivities: Many autistic individuals experience sensory sensitivities. This means they may be hyper-sensitive to certain sensory stimuli, such as loud noises or bright lights, while seeking sensory input in other areas, like rocking or stimming. These sensitivities can have a profound impact on their daily lives.

5. Executive Functioning: Challenges in executive functioning, which includes skills like organization, planning, and impulse control, are common in autism. These challenges can affect an individual's ability to manage daily tasks and activities effectively.

Now, it's crucial to recognize that the autism spectrum isn't just about challenges. It's also about celebrating the strengths and unique abilities of autistic individuals. Many possess remarkable talents, such as an exceptional memory, a deep passion for specific subjects, or a keen eye for detail.

In conclusion, the autism spectrum is a complex and beautifully diverse landscape, and it's important to approach it with empathy and a deep understanding of its many dimensions. This understanding is the foundation for providing effective and inclusive support for autistic learners.

Common Characteristics and Challenges in Autism

Understanding the common characteristics and challenges faced by autistic individuals is pivotal in providing effective support. It's essential to approach this topic with empathy and a deep appreciation for the unique experiences that each individual brings to the table.

1. Communication Differences: One of the most prevalent challenges in autism is differences in communication. Many autistic individuals face difficulties in understanding and using verbal and non-verbal communication. This can range from limited or absent speech to challenges in maintaining conversations and interpreting social cues.

2. Social Interaction: Autism often involves challenges in social interaction. This can manifest as struggles with forming and maintaining relationships, understanding social norms, or recognizing and responding to emotions in others. However, it's important to note that the degree of these challenges varies widely.

3. Repetitive Behaviors: Repetitive behaviors and interests are a common characteristic of autism. These can include rituals, routines, or intense interests in specific topics. These behaviors often serve as a way for individuals to cope with the world and find comfort in predictability.

4. Sensory Sensitivities: Many autistic individuals experience sensory sensitivities. They may be hypersensitive to sensory input, leading to discomfort or distress in response to certain sounds, lights, textures, or smells. On the other hand, some seek sensory input and engage in self-stimulatory behaviors like rocking or hand-flapping.

5. Executive Functioning Challenges: Executive functioning refers to a set of cognitive skills that enable individuals to plan, organize, and manage tasks. Many autistic individuals face challenges in this area, which can affect their ability to initiate and complete daily activities.

6. Specialized Interests and Strengths: While challenges are an integral part of autism, it's equally important to recognize the unique strengths and talents that many autistic individuals possess. They may excel in specific areas like mathematics, music, art, or have an exceptional memory.

7. Routine and Predictability: Autistic individuals often thrive in environments with routines and predictability. Sudden changes or

transitions can be challenging,
leading to anxiety or resistance.

8. Communication Support:
Providing alternative communication
methods, such as augmentative and
alternative communication (AAC) or
visual supports, can greatly assist
individuals who face verbal
communication challenges.

9. Sensory Accommodations: Making
accommodations for sensory
sensitivities is crucial. This may
involve providing sensory-friendly
spaces or offering noise-canceling
headphones.

10. Individualized Approaches:
Recognizing the unique profile of
each autistic individual is key. An

individualized approach ensures that support is tailored to their specific strengths and challenges.

In conclusion, common characteristics and challenges in autism are as diverse as the individuals themselves. This nuanced understanding is the foundation for providing meaningful and effective support to autistic individuals. It's about embracing the uniqueness of each individual and tailoring support to help them thrive in their own way.

Autism's Impact on Learning

Autism, as a neurodevelopmental condition, has a significant influence on the way individuals learn and engage with the world around them. It's important to approach this topic with empathy and a deep appreciation of the unique learning styles and needs of autistic learners.

1. Variability in Learning Styles: Autistic individuals often have diverse learning styles. Some may be visual learners, relying on visual aids and cues for comprehension, while others may benefit from more hands-on or experiential learning approaches. Recognizing and accommodating these differences is key to effective teaching.

2. Sensory Sensitivities: Sensory sensitivities, a common feature of autism, can greatly impact learning. An individual who is hypersensitive to certain sensory stimuli may become overwhelmed in a noisy classroom or an overly bright environment. Conversely, those seeking sensory input may engage in repetitive behaviors or stimming as a way to self-regulate.

3. Communication Challenges: Verbal and non-verbal communication difficulties can hinder the learning process. It may be challenging for autistic learners to express their needs, ask questions, or engage in classroom discussions. The use of alternative communication methods, such as visual supports or AAC, can greatly assist in bridging this gap.

4. Executive Functioning: Executive functioning skills, which include organization, time management, and impulse control, may be impaired in autistic individuals. These challenges can affect an individual's ability to initiate and complete tasks, manage their time effectively, and maintain organization in their work.

5. Specialized Interests and Strengths: Many autistic learners have specialized interests and strengths. These areas of passion can be leveraged to enhance learning experiences. Integrating an individual's interests into the curriculum can not only engage them more effectively but also provide opportunities for deep learning.

6. Support for Social Skills: The development of social skills is a critical component of learning. Autistic individuals may need additional support and guidance in this area to foster peer relationships and navigate social interactions.

7. Routine and Predictability: Routines and predictability are often essential for successful learning. Sudden changes or disruptions can be distressing for autistic learners, so providing a structured and consistent learning environment is crucial.

8. Individualized Education Plans (IEPs): Creating and implementing individualized education plans that are tailored to the specific needs and strengths of each autistic learner is a cornerstone of effective education. These plans should address communication, sensory accommodations, and executive functioning challenges, among others.

9. Inclusive Strategies: Inclusion in the classroom is paramount. Autistic learners should have access to inclusive education, where their unique needs are considered, and they are provided with the necessary supports to participate and thrive.

In summary, autism's impact on learning is multifaceted. Recognizing the diverse learning styles, sensory sensitivities, and communication challenges that autistic learners face is the first step toward providing effective and inclusive education. It's about fostering a learning environment that values neurodiversity and tailoring support to unlock the full potential of each learner.

Chapter 2: Effective Communication Strategies

Enhancing Communication Skills

Effective communication is a fundamental aspect of human interaction, and when it comes to working with autistic learners, it takes on an even greater significance. It's essential to approach this topic with empathy, patience, and a commitment to empowering autistic individuals to express themselves effectively.

1. Communication Challenges: Autistic learners may face a range of communication challenges. Some may have limited or absent speech, while others may struggle with expressive language, making it challenging for them to convey their thoughts and needs.

2. Alternative Communication Methods: It's crucial to recognize and support alternative communication methods. Augmentative and alternative communication (AAC) systems, such as picture exchange systems or speech-generating devices, can be invaluable in helping non-verbal or minimally verbal individuals express themselves.

3. Visual Supports: Visual supports, such as visual schedules, social stories, and visual cues, can enhance communication. They provide structure and predictability, making it easier for learners to understand and participate in various activities and social interactions.

4. Social Communication Skills: Teaching social communication skills is a vital component. This includes understanding non-verbal cues, recognizing emotions in others, and engaging in reciprocal conversations. Role-playing and social skills training can be beneficial in this regard.

5. Individualized Communication Plans: Recognize that each autistic learner is unique, and their communication needs will differ. Creating individualized communication plans that consider their strengths and challenges is essential. These plans should outline specific goals and strategies.

6. Communication Partners: Effective communication involves not only the individual but also their communication partners, which may include educators, tutors, and peers. It's essential to train and educate communication partners to adapt to the needs and preferences of the learner.

7. Patience and Active Listening: Patience is a virtue in enhancing communication skills. Actively listen to what the learner is trying to convey, even if their mode of communication is unconventional. Acknowledge their efforts and provide positive reinforcement.

8. Reducing Sensory Overload: Sensory sensitivities can interfere with communication. Create an environment that minimizes sensory overload by controlling noise, light, and other sensory stimuli that might be distracting or distressing.

9. Non-Judgmental Environment: Foster a non-judgmental and accepting communication environment. Autistic learners should feel safe to express themselves without fear of criticism or ridicule.

10. Building on Interests: Leveraging the learner's interests can be a powerful tool in enhancing communication. Incorporate their passions into learning and communication activities to increase motivation and engagement.

11. Building Vocabulary and Language Skills: Work on expanding vocabulary and language skills at an individualized pace. This may involve speech therapy, using communication apps, or other structured language interventions.

12. AAC Devices: For those who rely on AAC devices, ensure they have access to and training on these devices. AAC can provide a voice for individuals who may otherwise struggle to express themselves.

In conclusion, enhancing communication skills for autistic learners is a journey that requires patience, understanding, and a commitment to celebrating each individual's unique voice. It's about creating a communication-rich environment where every learner has the opportunity to express themselves and be heard, fostering a sense of empowerment and self-confidence.

The Importance of Visual Aids: A Comprehensive Perspective

Visual aids are an invaluable tool in education, and when it comes to working with autistic learners, their significance takes on an even more profound meaning. Understanding the role of visual aids in enhancing learning is essential for providing effective support.

1. Visual Learners: Many autistic learners are visual thinkers. They process and retain information more effectively when it's presented visually. Visual aids, such as charts, graphs, and images, cater to this learning style, making it easier for them to grasp and remember concepts.

2. Structure and Predictability: Visual supports, like visual schedules or social stories, provide structure and predictability in a world that can sometimes feel chaotic to autistic individuals. These tools offer a clear and organized way to understand what to expect, reducing anxiety and increasing a sense of control.

3. Communication: Visual aids serve as a powerful communication tool. For non-verbal or minimally verbal learners, communication boards and picture exchange systems enable them to express their needs and desires. Visual cues can also help in understanding and responding to social communication.

4. Reducing Sensory Overload: Autistic learners often experience sensory sensitivities. Visual aids can simplify and clarify complex verbal information, reducing the cognitive load and potential sensory overload during instruction.

5. Enhancing Independence: Visual supports can promote independence. A well-structured visual schedule, for example, allows learners to navigate their day with minimal assistance, fostering a sense of self-sufficiency.

6. Behavior Management: Visual supports play a key role in behavior management. Visual cues, like a "first-then" chart, can help learners understand the sequence of activities, reducing frustration and challenging behaviors.

7. Generalization of Skills: Visual aids assist in generalizing skills learned in one setting to others. A skill or concept taught with visual supports in the classroom can be more readily applied in different environments, including at home.

8. Individualization: The beauty of visual aids is their adaptability. They can be customized to meet the unique needs of each learner, reflecting their interests and challenges. This individualization ensures that the visual supports are highly relevant and effective.

9. Enhanced Communication Partner Skills: Visual aids also benefit communication partners, such as educators and caregivers. They provide a structured and consistent approach to communication, making it easier for partners to support and interact with learners effectively.

10. Self-Regulation: Visual supports help learners self-regulate their behavior and emotions. Visual cues, like a "calm down" chart, can guide learners in identifying and managing their emotional state.

11. Goal Setting: Visual aids can be used to set and track goals. Individuals can see their progress and understand what's expected of them, enhancing motivation and achievement.

In conclusion, the importance of visual aids in supporting autistic learners cannot be overstated. Visual supports provide structure, enhance communication, reduce sensory overload, and empower individuals to navigate their world with greater confidence and understanding. They are a means of fostering independence, promoting positive behaviors, and tailoring education to each learner's unique profile. Visual

aids are a powerful tool that
empowers both learners and their
support network.

Tips for Building Rapport with Autistic Learners: A Comprehensive Approach

Building a strong and trusting relationship with autistic learners is a cornerstone of effective teaching. It's essential to approach this topic with empathy, patience, and a genuine commitment to understanding and connecting with each individual.

1. Respect Individuality: Recognize that each autistic learner is unique. They have their own preferences, strengths, and challenges. Take the time to understand their specific needs and adapt your approach accordingly.

2. Active Listening: Practice active listening by giving your full attention when the learner communicates, whether verbally or through alternative methods. This shows that you value and respect their input.

3. Non-Verbal Cues: Be mindful of your own non-verbal cues. Autistic individuals often pay close attention to body language and facial expressions. Maintain open and approachable body language to convey warmth and receptivity.

4. Consistency and Predictability: Autistic learners thrive in environments that offer consistency and predictability. Establish routines and provide clear expectations to reduce anxiety and promote a sense of safety.

5. Visual Supports: Visual supports, such as visual schedules, can assist in understanding daily routines and transitions. These tools can help learners prepare for what's to come and reduce stress.

6. Respect Communication Preferences: Respect the learner's communication preferences. If they use augmentative and alternative communication (AAC), provide support and patience in using these methods.

7. Shared Interests: Identify and engage with the learner's interests. Shared activities related to their passions can create common ground for interaction and foster a sense of connection.

8. Sensory Sensitivities: Be aware of sensory sensitivities. Create an environment that minimizes sensory overload and discomfort, which can hinder rapport-building.

9. Reinforce Positive Behaviors: Acknowledge and reinforce positive behaviors and efforts. Positive reinforcement can motivate and build self-esteem.

10. Empower Choice: Give the learner choices whenever possible. Autonomy in decision-making can increase their sense of control and independence.

11. Social Stories: Social stories can be an effective way to prepare learners for new situations or social interactions. These stories provide clear and visual explanations of what to expect.

12. Patience: Building rapport may take time. Be patient and allow the learner to set the pace for interactions and comfort levels.

13. Collaborate with Caregivers: Work closely with caregivers or parents to understand the learner's background and unique needs. Collaboration and shared strategies ensure consistency in support.

14. Cultural Competence: Recognize and respect cultural diversity within the learner's family. Cultural competence is essential for understanding and accommodating the values and beliefs of the learner's family.

15. Celebrate Achievements: Celebrate even the small achievements. Positive recognition and encouragement can be incredibly motivating.

In conclusion, building rapport with autistic learners is a journey of understanding, patience, and genuine connection. It's about creating a supportive and inclusive learning environment where each learner feels valued and empowered. These tips are not just about teaching; they're about fostering trust, respect, and a positive learning experience for each individual.

Chapter 3: Creating a Supportive Learning Environment

Structuring the Tutoring Space for Autistic Learners: A Comprehensive Guide

The physical environment plays a significant role in the success of tutoring sessions with autistic learners. It's crucial to approach this topic with empathy, an understanding of sensory sensitivities, and a commitment to creating a conducive and supportive space for learning.

1. Sensory Considerations: Begin by assessing and addressing sensory sensitivities. Autistic learners may be hypersensitive to certain stimuli, such as bright lights, loud noises, or specific textures. Provide adjustable lighting, noise-cancelling headphones, and comfortable seating to accommodate sensory needs.

2. Clear Organization: Maintain a clear and organized tutoring space. Utilize visual supports, such as visual schedules or labels, to create predictability and reduce anxiety for the learner.

3. Minimal Distractions: Minimize distractions in the environment. Ensure that the tutoring space is free from unnecessary visual and auditory stimuli. This allows the learner to focus more effectively.

4. Visual Supports: Incorporate visual supports within the space. Visual schedules, communication boards, and visual cues can aid in communication and understanding of expectations.

5. Individualized Spaces: Consider the individual needs of each learner. Some may benefit from a private space with minimal sensory input, while others may thrive in a more open and social environment. Tailor the space to their specific preferences.

6. Comfort and Flexibility: Ensure that the seating and furniture are comfortable and adjustable. Autistic learners may have specific sensory preferences, and providing options can enhance their comfort and focus.

7. Organized Materials: Keep materials organized and easily accessible. Labeling containers and using visual cues for item placement can help the learner find what they need.

8. Communication Supports: Be sure to have augmentative and alternative communication (AAC) devices or boards available for those who rely

on non-verbal communication
methods.

9. Personalized Visual Supports:
Create visual supports that are
tailored to the learner's needs and
strengths. This may include visual
schedules with their preferred
activities or special interests.

10. Collaborative Spaces: Depending
on the learner's preferences,
consider spaces for collaborative
activities with peers. These spaces
should also be well-organized and
free from sensory distractions.

11. Positive Reinforcement Area:
Designate an area within the space
for celebrating achievements and
providing positive reinforcement.

This can motivate and create a positive learning atmosphere.

12. Calm-Down Corner: Include a designated calm-down corner where learners can retreat when feeling overwhelmed or overstimulated. This area should have sensory soothing tools, like fidget toys or sensory-friendly items.

13. Personalization: Allow the learner to personalize their space to some extent. Allowing them to bring in items of comfort or interest can help them feel more at ease.

14. Regular Updates: Continually assess the effectiveness of the tutoring space. Ask for feedback from the learner and their caregivers to make necessary adjustments.

In conclusion, structuring the tutoring space for autistic learners is about creating a welcoming, organized, and sensory-friendly environment that supports their unique needs and preferences. It's an investment in facilitating effective learning and providing a positive and inclusive space for each individual.

Sensory Considerations and Accommodations: A Comprehensive Approach

Understanding and addressing sensory sensitivities is a critical component of providing effective support for autistic learners. It's important to approach this topic with empathy and a deep commitment to creating a sensory-friendly environment that promotes comfort and learning.

1. Sensory Profiles: Begin by understanding the sensory profile of each learner. Recognize whether they are hypersensitive (overresponsive) or hyposensitive (under responsive) to sensory stimuli. This understanding forms the basis for personalized accommodations.

2. Sensory Breaks: Provide opportunities for sensory breaks. Designate a specific area or corner where learners can retreat when feeling overwhelmed or overstimulated. This space should include sensory tools like fidget toys, weighted blankets, or sensory-friendly items.

3. Sensory-Friendly Lighting: Utilize adjustable and sensory-friendly lighting. Natural lighting and dimmable options can reduce the impact of harsh fluorescent lighting that may be distressing to some learners.

4. Noise Control: Manage noise levels effectively. Noise-cancelling headphones or earplugs can help learners reduce auditory distractions. Use rugs or sound-dampening materials to minimize echo and reverberation in the space.

5. Preferred Sensory Inputs: Identify and incorporate sensory inputs that are preferred by the learner. Some may benefit from sensory tools like sensory swings, tactile textures, or calming sensory bottles.

6. Calming Sensory Tools: Provide access to calming sensory tools, such as stress balls, sensory brushes, or

calming scents like lavender. These
can help learners regulate their
sensory experiences.

7. Individualized Sensory Diets:

Develop individualized sensory diets.
These are specific activities or tools
that can help regulate a learner's
sensory needs. For instance, deep
pressure activities or sensory breaks
with specific sensory tools can be
part of the plan.

8. Predictable Sensory Input:

Maintain a predictable sensory
environment. Avoid sudden or
intense sensory input that might
cause distress. Create a
sensory-friendly routine that learners
can anticipate.

9. Sensory-Friendly Seating: Ensure that seating is comfortable and adjustable. Some learners may prefer flexible seating options, like stability balls or wobble stools, to meet their sensory needs.

10. Visual Supports: Use visual supports to prepare learners for sensory experiences, transitions, or changes in the environment. Visual schedules can provide a clear and structured understanding of the sensory aspect of the day.

11. Gradual Exposure: When introducing new sensory experiences or activities, do so gradually and with the learner's consent. This reduces anxiety and allows them to adjust at their own pace.

12. Regular Feedback: Continuously seek feedback from the learner and their caregivers. They can provide insights into sensory experiences and help tailor accommodations effectively.

In conclusion, sensory considerations and accommodations are an essential part of providing support for autistic learners. It's about creating a sensory-friendly environment that recognizes the unique sensory profiles of each individual and tailors support to enhance their comfort and well-being. This approach fosters a positive and inclusive learning

atmosphere that empowers each
learner to thrive.

Managing Sensory Overload: A Comprehensive Approach

Sensory overload can be overwhelming and distressing for autistic learners, and it's essential to approach this topic with empathy and a deep commitment to helping them navigate their sensory experiences effectively.

1. Sensory Awareness: Start by developing sensory awareness. Recognize the specific sensory sensitivities of each learner. This understanding is the foundation for managing sensory overload.

2. Communication: Encourage open and effective communication. Teach learners to express their sensory discomfort or overwhelm. This empowers them to seek assistance when needed.

3. Sensory Breaks: Provide designated sensory break areas where learners can retreat when they feel overloaded. These areas should be equipped with sensory tools that help them self-regulate, like fidget toys or sensory swings.

4. Calm-Down Strategies: Teach learners effective calm-down strategies. These may include deep breathing exercises, mindfulness techniques, or using sensory tools like stress balls or weighted blankets.

5. Visual Schedules: Use visual schedules to prepare learners for sensory experiences. Visual cues can help them anticipate and mentally prepare for situations that may cause sensory discomfort.

6. Noise Control: Manage noise levels effectively. Use noise-cancelling headphones or earplugs to minimize auditory overload. When possible, create quiet spaces for learners to escape noisy environments.

7. Predictable Routines: Maintain consistent and predictable routines. Knowing what to expect can reduce

anxiety and make sensory
experiences more manageable.

8. Sensory Tools: Ensure that sensory
tools are readily available. These
tools can include sensory brushes,
tactile textures, or sensory-friendly
items that offer comfort and
grounding during overwhelming
moments.

9. Sensory-Friendly Lighting: Utilize
adjustable and sensory-friendly
lighting. Dimmable or natural lighting
options can help create a more
comfortable sensory environment.

10. Clear Communication: Educate
caregivers, educators, and peers on
the signs of sensory overload and
how to provide support. Clear

communication ensures a collaborative effort in managing sensory challenges.

11. Individualized Plans: Develop individualized sensory plans that outline specific sensory triggers and coping strategies. This ensures that the learner's unique needs are addressed.

12. Gradual Exposure: When introducing new sensory experiences or activities, do so gradually and with the learner's consent. This approach allows them to adjust to new sensory input at their own pace.

13. Non-Judgmental Environment: Create a non-judgmental and accepting environment where learners feel safe to express their sensory discomfort and seek assistance without fear of criticism.

14. Self-Regulation Techniques: Teach learners self-regulation techniques that they can apply independently. These strategies provide them with a sense of control over their sensory experiences.

In conclusion, managing sensory overload is about creating a supportive and inclusive environment that empowers autistic learners to regulate their sensory experiences effectively. It's about recognizing the unique sensory sensitivities of each individual and providing them with the tools and strategies to navigate

their sensory world with confidence
and comfort.

Chapter 4: Individualized Teaching Approaches

Tailoring Lessons to the Student's Needs: A Comprehensive Guide

Adapting lessons to accommodate the specific needs and learning styles of autistic learners is essential for effective education. It's important to approach this topic with empathy, patience, and a commitment to providing a meaningful and inclusive learning experience.

1. Individualized Education Plans (IEPs): Start by reviewing the learner's Individualized Education Plan (IEP), if applicable. This document outlines the specific goals and accommodations necessary to meet their needs.

2. Sensory Considerations: Understand the learner's sensory sensitivities. Tailor the environment to minimize sensory distractions and provide sensory supports as needed.

3. Visual Supports: Utilize visual supports to enhance understanding. Visual schedules, social stories, and visual cues can assist in explaining concepts and providing structure to the lesson.

4. Simplify Language: Use clear and concise language when delivering instructions. Avoid figurative language and idioms that may be confusing.

5. Break Down Complex Tasks: Divide complex tasks into smaller, manageable steps. This approach makes learning more achievable and reduces frustration.

6. Provide Visual and Written Instructions: Offer both verbal and written instructions to cater to different learning styles. Written instructions can serve as a reference for the learner.

7. Individualized Goals: Set individualized learning goals that align with the learner's strengths and challenges. Celebrate their progress, no matter how small, as this can be highly motivating.

8. Incorporate Special Interests: Integrate the learner's special interests into the curriculum. Using these interests as a bridge to learning can enhance engagement and motivation.

9. Allow for Processing Time: Be patient and allow the learner sufficient processing time. Autistic individuals may need extra time to understand and respond to information.

10. Varied Instructional Methods: Employ a variety of instructional methods. Some learners may benefit from visual aids, while others may respond better to hands-on or experiential learning.

11. Promote Independence:

Encourage the development of independent skills. Teach self-regulation, organization, and problem-solving to foster greater independence.

12. Regular Feedback and Assessment:

Provide regular feedback and assessments to gauge the learner's understanding. Adjust the teaching approach based on their progress and needs.

13. Collaborate with Caregivers:

Work closely with caregivers to share

insights and strategies that work well for the learner at home. This collaboration ensures consistency in support.

14. Foster Social Skills: Include opportunities for social interaction and the development of social skills within lessons. Group activities can help learners practice communication and cooperation.

15. Positive Reinforcement: Use positive reinforcement to acknowledge and reward the learner's efforts and achievements. This can motivate and build self-esteem.

In conclusion, tailoring lessons to the needs of autistic learners is about creating a learning environment that is flexible, supportive, and individualized. It's an investment in providing an education that respects the unique profile of each learner and empowers them to reach their full potential.

Using Applied Behavior Analysis (ABA) Principles: A Comprehensive Approach

Applied Behavior Analysis (ABA) is a valuable approach for supporting autistic learners, and when used effectively, it can greatly enhance their development. It's important to approach this topic with empathy, understanding, and a commitment to applying ABA principles in a manner that respects the learner's unique needs.

1. Individualized Assessment: Start with an individualized assessment of the learner's strengths, challenges, and goals. This assessment forms the basis for tailoring ABA interventions.

2. Data Collection: ABA relies on data collection to track progress. Use systematic data collection methods to monitor the learner's behaviors and responses to interventions.

3. Set Clear and Measurable Goals: Establish clear and measurable goals that are tailored to the learner's needs. These goals should be specific and achievable within a defined timeframe.

4. Positive Reinforcement: Implement positive reinforcement strategies to motivate and reinforce desired behaviors. Identify the learner's preferred reinforcers and use them effectively.

5. Prompting and Fading: Use prompting to support the learner in acquiring new skills. Gradually fade prompts as the learner becomes more independent and proficient in the targeted behavior.

6. Errorless Learning: Employ errorless learning techniques to minimize mistakes and maximize success. This reduces frustration and builds confidence.

7. Task Analysis: Break down complex tasks into smaller, sequential steps. Task analysis allows the learner to master one aspect of a skill before progressing to the next.

8. Generalization: Teach skills in multiple settings to promote generalization. Ensure that the learner can apply what they've learned in different environments and with different people.

9. Discrete Trial Teaching: Use discrete trial teaching to structure teaching trials and provide immediate feedback. This approach is particularly useful for teaching new skills.

10. Functional Communication Training: Implement functional communication training to help the learner express their needs and wants effectively. This reduces challenging behaviors and promotes independence.

11. Visual Supports: Incorporate visual supports, such as visual schedules or token boards, to enhance communication and understanding of expectations.

12. Collaboration with Caregivers: Collaborate closely with caregivers and family members to ensure consistency in implementing ABA strategies across different settings.

13. Behavior Reduction: If challenging behaviors are a concern, apply behavior reduction techniques to address and reduce these behaviors effectively. These should be based on functional assessments.

14. Ethical Considerations: Ensure that ABA interventions are implemented in an ethical and respectful manner. Respect the autonomy and dignity of the learner at all times.

15. Ongoing Evaluation: Continuously evaluate the effectiveness of ABA interventions and make necessary adjustments based on the learner's progress and needs.

In conclusion, using ABA principles with autistic learners is about providing structured, data-driven, and individualized support that fosters growth and independence. It's an approach that, when applied with empathy and respect, can empower each learner to achieve their goals and maximize their potential.

Developing IEPs and Personalized Goals: A Comprehensive Approach

Creating Individualized Education Plans (IEPs) and personalized goals is a fundamental aspect of providing effective support for autistic learners. It's important to approach this topic with empathy, understanding, and a commitment to tailoring education to each learner's unique needs.

1. Comprehensive Assessment: Begin with a comprehensive assessment of the learner. This should include evaluations of their academic, social, communication, sensory, and behavioral needs. Involve caregivers, educators, and specialists in this process.

2. Clear and Measurable Goals: Establish clear and measurable goals based on the assessment. Goals should be specific, achievable, and individualized to address the learner's unique strengths and challenges.

3. SMART Goals: Ensure that goals are SMART—Specific, Measurable, Achievable, Relevant, and Time-bound. SMART goals provide a clear framework for tracking progress.

4. Collaborative Team: Involve a collaborative team in the development of the IEP. This team may include educators, speech therapists, occupational therapists, behavior analysts, and caregivers. Collaboration ensures a well-rounded and informed approach.

5. Prioritization: Prioritize goals based on the learner's immediate needs and long-term objectives. Focus on the most critical areas that require support.

6. Individualized Accommodations: Identify and include individualized accommodations and modifications to support the learner's access to the curriculum. These may involve sensory supports, communication tools, or behavioral interventions.

7. Behavior Support Plans: If the learner exhibits challenging behaviors, create behavior support plans that include functional assessments, interventions, and crisis management strategies.

8. Communication Supports: Integrate communication supports into the IEP. For non-verbal or minimally verbal learners, augmentative and alternative communication (AAC) systems should be included.

9. Social Skills Development: If social skills are a concern, outline specific goals for developing social communication and interaction skills.

Consider peer interactions and relationship-building.

10. Transition Planning: Include transition planning for learners who are approaching significant life changes, such as transitioning from school to post-secondary education or the workforce. These plans should focus on fostering independence and life skills.

11. Progress Monitoring: Implement systematic data collection and progress monitoring methods to track the learner's development and adapt the IEP as needed.

12. Regular IEP Meetings: Schedule regular IEP meetings with the collaborative team to review progress, discuss challenges, and make adjustments to the plan. These meetings provide a platform for open communication and continuous improvement.

13. Family Involvement: Involve the learner's family in the development and ongoing implementation of the IEP. Family input is invaluable for tailoring support effectively.

14. High Expectations: Maintain high expectations for the learner's potential. Ensure that the IEP promotes growth and independence, rather than setting limits on their capabilities.

15. Ethical Considerations: Ensure that the IEP is developed and implemented in an ethical and respectful manner. Uphold the learner's autonomy and dignity throughout the process.

In conclusion, developing IEPs and personalized goals for autistic learners is about creating a dynamic and flexible roadmap that addresses their unique needs and aspirations. It's an investment in providing tailored support that empowers each learner to achieve their full potential and thrive.

Chapter 5: Behavior Management Techniques

Understanding Challenging Behaviors: A Comprehensive Approach

Autistic learners may exhibit challenging behaviors, and it's essential to approach this topic with empathy, patience, and a commitment to understanding the underlying causes and triggers for these behaviors.

1. Functional Assessment: Begin by conducting a functional assessment to understand the purpose or function of the challenging behavior. This involves identifying the triggers and consequences associated with the behavior.

**2. Communication: Challenging behaviors can often be a form of communication for autistic learners. Recognize that these behaviors may be an attempt to express needs, discomfort, or frustration.

3. Sensory Sensitivities: Some challenging behaviors may stem from sensory sensitivities. Identify sensory triggers and consider how to provide sensory accommodations or alternatives.

4. Anxiety and Overload: Anxiety and sensory overload can lead to challenging behaviors. Help learners develop self-regulation and coping strategies to manage these feelings effectively.

5. Social and Communication Challenges: Difficulty with social interactions and communication can contribute to challenging behaviors. Support the development of social skills and alternative communication methods.

6. Behavior Intervention Plan (BIP): If the challenging behavior persists, develop a Behavior Intervention Plan

(BIP). This plan outlines strategies for addressing and reducing the behavior, such as replacement behaviors and positive reinforcement.

7. Antecedent Modifications: Modify the environment to prevent or minimize antecedents (triggers) for challenging behaviors. This may include reducing sensory overload or changing routines to make them more predictable.

8. Positive Behavior Support: Implement positive behavior support strategies to reinforce appropriate behaviors and reduce challenging ones. Positive reinforcement and reward systems can be effective in this regard.

9. Training and Skill Development: Provide training and skill development in areas where the learner may struggle. This includes social skills training, communication training, and emotional regulation techniques.

10. Collaboration: Collaborate with a team of professionals, caregivers, and educators to develop a comprehensive approach to addressing challenging behaviors. Everyone involved should be informed and supportive.

11. Functional Communication Training: Consider functional communication training to help the learner express their needs and wants effectively, reducing frustration and challenging behaviors.

12. Individualized Strategies: Recognize that challenging behaviors are highly individualized. Tailor interventions and strategies to address the specific triggers and underlying causes for each learner.

13. Ethical Considerations: Ensure that interventions and strategies are applied in an ethical and respectful manner, respecting the learner's dignity and autonomy at all times.

14. Data Collection: Continuously collect data to monitor the progress of behavior interventions. This data helps in evaluating the effectiveness of strategies and making necessary adjustments.

15. Patience and Consistency: Be patient and consistent in applying interventions. Behavior change takes time, and learners may need support and reinforcement to develop new, more adaptive behaviors.

In conclusion, understanding challenging behaviors in autistic learners is about identifying the underlying causes, providing appropriate support, and fostering positive change. It's an approach that aims to help learners express themselves effectively, reduce anxiety and sensory overload, and

develop the skills they need to
navigate the world with confidence.

Strategies for Behavior Intervention: A Comprehensive Approach

Behavior intervention strategies are essential for addressing challenging behaviors in autistic learners, and it's crucial to approach this topic with empathy, patience, and a commitment to helping the learner develop more adaptive and positive behaviors.

1. Functional Assessment: Begin with a functional assessment to understand the underlying causes and functions of the challenging behavior. This involves identifying the triggers and consequences associated with the behavior.

2. Behavior Intervention Plan (BIP): Develop a Behavior Intervention Plan (BIP) based on the findings from the functional assessment. This plan outlines specific strategies and interventions to address and reduce the challenging behavior.

3. Replacement Behaviors: Identify and teach replacement behaviors that serve the same function as the challenging behavior but are more socially appropriate. For example, if the learner engages in hitting as a form of communication, teach them alternative ways to express their needs or frustrations.

4. Positive Reinforcement:
Implement positive reinforcement strategies to motivate and reinforce desired behaviors. Identify the learner's preferred reinforcers and use them effectively to encourage appropriate conduct.

5. Visual Supports: Utilize visual supports, such as visual schedules, token boards, or social stories, to help the learner understand expectations and consequences related to their behavior.

6. Self-Regulation Techniques: Teach the learner self-regulation techniques, such as deep breathing, mindfulness, or sensory-based

strategies, to manage their emotions
and behavior effectively.

**7. Functional Communication
Training:** If the challenging behavior
is related to communication
difficulties, use functional
communication training to help the
learner express their needs and
wants more effectively.

8. Collaboration: Collaborate with a
team of professionals, caregivers, and
educators to develop and implement
the BIP. A team approach ensures a
comprehensive and informed
strategy.

9. Environmental Modifications:
Modify the environment to prevent
or minimize antecedents (triggers) for

challenging behaviors. This may include reducing sensory overload, simplifying tasks, or adjusting routines.

10. Data Collection: Continuously collect data to monitor the effectiveness of behavior interventions. Data helps in evaluating progress and making necessary adjustments to the BIP.

11. Ethical Considerations: Ensure that behavior interventions are implemented in an ethical and respectful manner, respecting the learner's dignity and autonomy at all times.

12. Communication and Feedback: Maintain open communication with the learner and their caregivers. Seek feedback and insights to refine and improve behavior interventions.

13. Crisis Management: Develop crisis management strategies for handling challenging behaviors in emergency situations. These strategies should prioritize safety and de-escalation.

14. Individualization: Recognize that behavior intervention strategies must be highly individualized. Tailor interventions to address the specific triggers and functions of challenging behaviors for each learner.

15. Patience and Consistency: Be patient and consistent in applying behavior interventions. Positive behavior change takes time, and learners may need ongoing support to develop new, more adaptive behaviors.

In conclusion, behavior intervention strategies are about identifying the causes of challenging behaviors and implementing effective, individualized strategies to encourage positive change. It's an approach that aims to help learners express themselves more effectively, manage their emotions, and develop the skills they need to interact with the world in a constructive and adaptive manner.

Positive Reinforcement and De-escalation Methods: A Comprehensive Approach

Positive reinforcement and de-escalation methods are essential tools for promoting positive behavior and managing challenging situations with autistic learners. It's crucial to approach this topic with empathy, patience, and a commitment to creating a supportive and calming environment.

Positive Reinforcement:

1. Identify Preferred Reinforcers: Begin by identifying the learner's preferred reinforcers, such as specific activities, items, or social interactions. These are the rewards that motivate the learner.

2. Use Reinforcement Schedules: Implement reinforcement schedules, which can include immediate reinforcement for small achievements and delayed reinforcement for larger accomplishments. This helps maintain motivation.

3. Reinforce Desired Behaviors: Consistently reinforce desired behaviors. Acknowledge and reward the learner when they exhibit positive conduct. Be specific in your praise, describing the behavior you're reinforcing.

4. Shaping: Use shaping to gradually build complex skills. Reward successive approximations of the target behavior, reinforcing small steps toward the desired outcome.

5. Social Reinforcement: Whenever possible, use social reinforcement in the form of praise, positive attention, or interaction with peers. Many autistic learners respond positively to social rewards.

6. Token Systems: Implement token systems where learners can earn tokens for desired behaviors. These tokens can be exchanged for a preferred item or activity, providing motivation.

7. Individualized Approach: Tailor reinforcement to the learner's individual preferences. What motivates one learner may not be effective for another, so be flexible in your approach.

De-escalation Methods:

8. Calming Environment: Create a calming environment by reducing sensory stimuli, dimming lights, and providing access to sensory tools that help the learner self-regulate.

9. Communication: Encourage the learner to communicate their feelings or needs when they are becoming distressed. Teach them alternative ways to express themselves to reduce frustration.

10. Predictable Routines: Maintain predictable routines and use visual supports to help the learner anticipate what comes next. Predictability reduces anxiety and provides a sense of security.

11. Calm-Down Corner: Designate a calm-down corner where the learner can retreat when feeling overwhelmed. Ensure this space contains sensory soothing tools and a comforting atmosphere.

12. Deep Breathing and Mindfulness: Teach deep breathing exercises and mindfulness techniques to help the learner manage stress and anxiety. These methods can be useful in de-escalating challenging situations.

13. Verbal De-escalation: Use verbal de-escalation techniques that involve speaking calmly, maintaining eye contact, and using a soothing tone of voice. Acknowledge the learner's feelings and empathize with their experiences.

14. Safe Physical Management: In rare cases where safety is a concern, use safe physical management techniques to ensure the safety of the learner and others. This should only be employed as a last resort and by trained professionals.

15. Crisis Prevention: Develop crisis prevention plans to identify triggers and proactively address them before escalation occurs. These plans help in preventing challenging behaviors from developing.

16. Team Collaboration: Collaborate with caregivers, educators, and professionals to establish consistent de-escalation strategies. Ensure that everyone involved is aware of and trained in these methods.

17. Ethical Considerations: Implement de-escalation methods in an ethical and respectful manner, prioritizing the dignity and autonomy of the learner.

In conclusion, positive reinforcement and de-escalation methods are about promoting positive behavior and creating a supportive, calming environment for autistic learners. These approaches aim to reinforce desired behaviors, manage challenging situations, and provide effective strategies for reducing stress and anxiety.

Chapter 6: Collaborating with Parents and Professionals

Building a Support Network: A Comprehensive Approach

Creating a robust support network is crucial for providing effective care and education for autistic learners. It's important to approach this topic with empathy, collaboration, and a commitment to surrounding the learner with a team of professionals, caregivers, and educators who can offer comprehensive support.

1. Collaborative Team: Assemble a collaborative team of professionals, caregivers, and educators who are knowledgeable about autism and dedicated to the learner's well-being. This team may include special education teachers, speech therapists, occupational therapists, behavior analysts, and medical professionals.

2. Clear Communication: Maintain open and clear communication among all team members. Regular meetings and discussions ensure that everyone is informed and aligned in their approach to support the learner.

3. Empower Caregivers: Empower caregivers and family members with the knowledge and skills they need to support the learner effectively. Offer training, resources, and guidance to build their capacity in providing care.

4. Specialized Professionals: Seek out professionals with expertise in autism spectrum disorders. These specialists can provide tailored interventions and strategies that align with the learner's unique needs.

5. Support Groups: Connect caregivers with support groups or networks of other families who have experience with autism. Peer support can be invaluable in sharing insights and coping strategies.

6. Individualized Plans:

Collaboratively develop individualized plans, such as Individualized Education Plans (IEPs) and Behavior Intervention Plans (BIPs), to ensure the learner's specific needs are addressed.

7. Regular Feedback: Encourage caregivers to provide regular feedback on the learner's progress, challenges, and any changes in their needs. This feedback helps in making necessary adjustments to support strategies.

8. Respite Care: Offer respite care services to caregivers, providing them with breaks and opportunities for self-care to prevent burnout.

9. Multidisciplinary Evaluations:
Arrange for multidisciplinary
evaluations to get a comprehensive
understanding of the learner's
strengths and challenges. This
informs the development of tailored
support.

10. Community Resources: Connect
with community resources, such as
autism organizations, advocacy
groups, and local service providers,
to access additional support and
information.

11. Inclusive Education: Promote
inclusive education by working
closely with mainstream educators
and schools to ensure that the

learner has access to a supportive and inclusive learning environment.

12. Professional Development: Ensure that all team members, including educators and caregivers, have access to ongoing professional development and training to stay updated on the latest research and practices in autism support.

13. Ethical Considerations: Uphold ethical considerations throughout the support network building process, respecting the autonomy and dignity of the learner and their caregivers.

14. Parent-Professional Partnerships: Foster strong parent-professional partnerships, where caregivers and educators collaborate as equal partners in the learner's care and education.

15. Transition Planning: Include transition planning in the support network for learners approaching significant life changes, such as transitioning from school to post-secondary education or the workforce.

In conclusion, building a support network for autistic learners is about creating a comprehensive and collaborative team that surrounds the learner with knowledge, care, and resources. This network empowers the learner to achieve their potential and ensures that they receive the best possible care and education.

Effective Communication with Caregivers: A Comprehensive Approach

Maintaining open and effective communication with caregivers is vital for the well-being and progress of autistic learners. It's essential to approach this topic with empathy, transparency, and a commitment to working together to support the learner effectively.

1. Regular Updates: Provide regular updates to caregivers about the learner's progress, challenges, and achievements. This can be done through meetings, emails, or a communication log.

2. Collaborative Planning: Involve caregivers in the planning and decision-making process. Collaboratively develop goals, strategies, and interventions that align with the learner's needs and preferences.

3. Active Listening: Practice active listening when caregivers express concerns, insights, or suggestions. Ensure that caregivers feel heard and valued as part of the support team.

4. Empathy: Approach interactions with caregivers with empathy and understanding. Recognize the unique challenges and experiences they face and validate their feelings and concerns.

5. Clear and Accessible Information: Provide clear and accessible information about the learner's educational plan, including Individualized Education Plans (IEPs), Behavior Intervention Plans (BIPs), and support strategies.

6. Training and Resources: Offer training and resources to caregivers to empower them with the knowledge and skills they need to support the learner effectively. This can include workshops, webinars, or written materials.

7. Feedback Channels: Establish clear feedback channels for caregivers to communicate their observations and concerns. Encourage them to share insights about the learner's behavior, progress, or any changes in their needs.

8. Regular Meetings: Schedule regular meetings with caregivers to discuss the learner's development, challenges, and any necessary adjustments to the support plan. These meetings provide opportunities for collaboration and alignment.

9. Goal Setting: Collaboratively set goals with caregivers to ensure that everyone is working toward common objectives. These goals should be specific, measurable, and tailored to the learner's needs.

10. Inclusive Approach: Promote an inclusive approach that involves caregivers as equal partners in the learner's care and education. Make them an integral part of the support network.

11. Support and Empowerment: Offer emotional support and empowerment to caregivers, acknowledging the demands and stresses they may face. Encourage self-care and provide respite care options.

12. Problem-Solving: Collaborate with caregivers in problem-solving when challenges arise. Encourage them to contribute ideas and strategies to address issues effectively.

13. Transition Planning: Include caregivers in transition planning when the learner is approaching significant life changes, such as transitioning from school to post-secondary education or the workforce.

14. Ethical Considerations: Uphold ethical considerations in all interactions with caregivers, respecting their autonomy and dignity and ensuring that their perspectives are valued.

15. Ongoing Communication: Ensure that communication is ongoing and not limited to specific events or meetings. Maintain a consistent and open channel for sharing information and insights.

In conclusion, effective communication with caregivers is about establishing a collaborative and supportive partnership that prioritizes the well-being and progress of the autistic learner. It's an approach that recognizes the valuable insights and contributions of caregivers and empowers them to play an active role in the learner's journey.

Teamwork for the Best Outcomes

Teamwork is the cornerstone of providing the best outcomes for autistic learners. It's essential to approach this topic with a commitment to collaboration, open communication, and a shared dedication to the learner's well-being and success.

1. Collaborative Approach: Embrace a collaborative approach that involves professionals, caregivers, and educators working together as a unified team. Recognize that each member brings unique expertise and insights to the table.

2. Regular Meetings: Schedule regular team meetings to discuss the learner's progress, challenges, and any necessary adjustments to support strategies. These meetings provide a platform for sharing information and insights.

3. Clear Roles and Responsibilities: Define clear roles and responsibilities for each team member. Ensure that everyone understands their specific contributions and commitments to the learner's support.

4. Open Communication: Maintain open and transparent communication among team members. Create a culture of trust where everyone feels comfortable sharing their observations and concerns.

5. Shared Goals: Establish shared goals and objectives for the learner's development. Ensure that these goals are specific, measurable, and tailored to the learner's individual needs.

6. Collaborative Decision-Making: Include all team members in the decision-making process. Collaboratively develop goals, strategies, and interventions that align with the learner's preferences and challenges.

7. Multidisciplinary Expertise: Recognize the value of multidisciplinary expertise. Team

members may include special
education teachers, speech
therapists, occupational therapists,
behavior analysts, and medical
professionals.

8. Consistency and Alignment:
Ensure that all team members are
aligned in their approach to support.
Consistency in interventions and
strategies is key to achieving the best
outcomes.

9. Empowerment: Empower
caregivers with the knowledge and
skills they need to play an active role
in the learner's support. Offer
training, resources, and emotional
support.

10. Problem-Solving: Collaboratively problem-solve when challenges arise. Encourage team members to contribute their ideas and insights to address issues effectively.

11. Ethical Considerations: Uphold ethical considerations in all team interactions. Respect the autonomy and dignity of the learner and their caregivers, ensuring that their perspectives are valued.

12. Positive Feedback: Provide positive feedback and acknowledgment to team members for their contributions and efforts. Recognize the value of their commitment to the learner's well-being.

13. Inclusive Education: Promote inclusive education by working closely with mainstream educators and schools to ensure that the learner has access to a supportive and inclusive learning environment.

14. Transition Planning: Include transition planning in the team's discussions when the learner is approaching significant life changes, such as transitioning from school to post-secondary education or the workforce.

15. Regular Training: Offer ongoing professional development and training to all team members to stay updated on the latest research and practices in autism support.

In conclusion, teamwork is the foundation for achieving the best outcomes for autistic learners. It's about leveraging the collective expertise, insights, and dedication of a collaborative team to provide the learner with the most comprehensive and effective support possible.